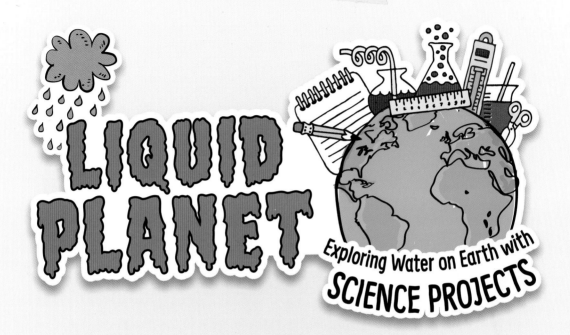

LIQUID PLANET

Exploring Water on Earth with
SCIENCE PROJECTS

by Tammy Enz

Raintree is an imprint of Capstone Global Library Limited, a company incorporated in England and Wales having its registered office at 7 Pilgrim Street, London, EC4V 6LB – Registered company number: 6695582

www.raintree.co.uk
myorders@raintree.co.uk

Edited by Alesha Sullivan
Designed by Sarah Bennett
Picture research by Kelly Garvin
Production by Lori Barbeau

ISBN 978 1 474 70325 3 (hardback)   ISBN 978 1 474 70330 7 (paperback)
19 18 17 16 15   20 19 18 17 16
10 9 8 7 6 5 4 3 2 1   10 9 8 7 6 5 4 3 2 1

British Library Cataloguing in Publication Data
A full catalogue record for this book is available from the British Library.

Acknowledgements
Captstone Press/Karon Dubke, 8, 9, 11, 12, 13 (left), 15, 16–17, 18, 19, 21 (right), 25, 28; Shutterstock: Africa Studio, 10, alybaba, 12–13, bogdan ionescu, 20–21, chaoss, 29, Charles Knowles, 22–23, EpicStockMedia, 26, ifong, 14, Jose Ignacio Soto, 6–7, Justin Black, 4–5, Maksym Darakchi, 17 (top inset), MarArt, 23, O.Guero, cover, stockshoppe, 7 (inset), violetkaipa, 27
Design Elements: Shutterstock: Curly Pat, Magnia, Markovka, Ms.Moloko, Orfeev, pockygallery, Sashatigar

We would like to thank Ginger L. Schmid, PhD, Associate Professor for the Department of Geography at Minnesota State University, Mankato, for her invaluable help in the preparation of this book.

Printed and bound in China.

Contents

Water on Earth

Can you imagine our planet without any water? There would be no summer time dips in the pool. You couldn't enjoy a refreshing glass of water after a day of playing at the park. But that's not all. Without water Earth would be a very different planet.

Most of Earth's surface is covered with water. But you'll also find water in the air, under the ground, in lakes and rivers and even inside of you. Scientists are busily searching the solar system for signs of water on other planets. Why? Life can only exist where there is water. So far Earth is the only planet where water is known to exist.

Did you know water is more than just a liquid? Water is solid when it becomes ice. As water **vapour** it is an invisible gas floating around the **atmosphere**. Would you like to take a closer look at water's role on Earth? Grab some supplies and dive into experiments that will teach you all about water! You may need an adult's help for some — think safety first!

Water is a vital building block for the human body. Your skin is about 64 per cent water. Your brain and heart are about 73 per cent water. Even your bones are nearly a third water!

vapour gas made from something that is usually a liquid or solid at normal temperatures

atmosphere mixture of gases that surrounds Earth

Sun, Earth and water

Water is found in obvious places, such as rivers and oceans. But did you know water is also inside plants and clouds? Water even forms pools in giant caves underground.

Water is constantly moving and changing its form. How does this moving and changing take place? Lots of processes are involved, as shown by the **water cycle**. With a few materials you can see how this cycle moves water between Earth and the sky.

water cycle how water changes as it travels around the world and moves between the ground and the air

The Water Cycle

Liquid water enters the atmosphere through **evaporation** or **transpiration**. In transpiration plants breathe out water vapour. The gaseous water cools in the air and **condenses** into clouds. When the clouds have gathered enough heavy water droplets, **precipitation** falls to the ground. Precipitation can be in the form of rain, snow or ice. Precipitation filters into the ground or runs into rivers and lakes. The water cycle process repeats over and over again.

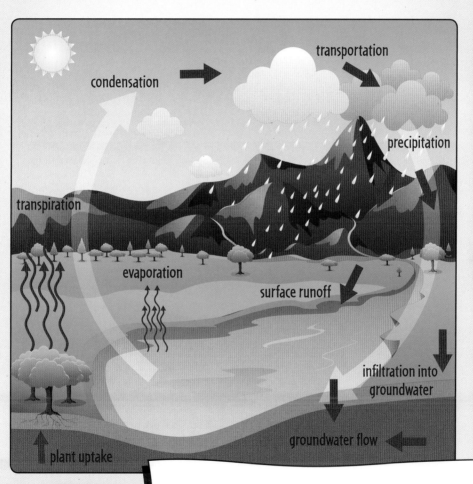

evaporate change from a liquid to a vapour or a gas

transpiration process in which plants give off moisture into the atmosphere

condense change from a gas to a liquid

precipitation water that falls from clouds to Earth's surface

What you do

What you need

sand

plastic container the size of a shoe box

water

small glass at least 2.5 centimetres (1 inch) shorter than the plastic container

cling film

tape

ice cubes

small bowl

clock or timer

1. Put 2.5 centimetres (1 inch) sand in the bottom of a plastic container.

2. Slowly pour water over the sand until the sand is damp. Stop pouring water when the sand no longer soaks up water. The sand represents Earth's surface.

3. Place a glass upright in the middle of the sand. Push it down into the sand.

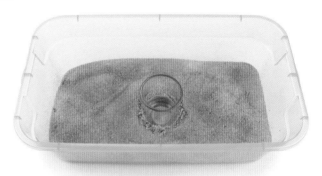

4. Cover the container with cling film. Tape the cling film securely to the sides of the container. The cling film should be as airtight as possible. The cling film represents Earth's atmosphere.

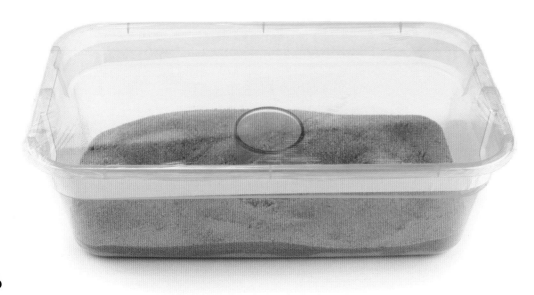

5. Place two or three ice cubes in a bowl. Place the bowl on the cling film, directly over the glass. Make sure there is a gap between the top of the glass and the bottom of the dish.

Helpful Hint: If the bowl touches the glass, try to adjust the cling film so it's tighter around the container.

6. Put the container in the sunshine for 30 minutes until the ice in the bowl melts.

7. Carefully remove the bowl and the cling film. Look inside the glass. What can you see? Where has the water moved to? Did the Sun's heat evaporate the water from the sand? You have created a simple water cycle!

A disappearing act

Have you ever wondered what happens to the puddles on a pavement after it's rained? After a few hours the puddles seem to disappear. This disappearing act is called evaporation. The rainwater that filled the puddle doesn't really disappear. The water simply takes on a different form. Evaporation uses the Sun's energy to change liquid water into a gas. Try this fun experiment — it's evaporation in action!

Sweaty?

Evaporation doesn't only happen to water on Earth. Water evaporates from you too. Sweating is an amazing process that helps to keep you cool. When your body sweats, the evaporation of the sweat droplets pulls heat away from your body, lowering your temperature. Dogs also sweat, but they have a different way of cooling down. As well as sweating from their paws, they pant. Panting causes water to evaporate off their tongues.

What you do

What you need

3 identical sponges

bucket of water

3 plastic plates

electric fan

electric hair-drier

clock or timer

1. Soak the sponges in a bucket of water. Pull each sponge out, and gently squeeze until no water drips out. The sponges should be damp.

2. Place each sponge in the middle of a plate.

3. Put one of the plates inside, somewhere where it won't be disturbed.

4. Place the second plate in front of a fan. Set the fan to the lowest setting.

5. Carefully blow heat onto the third plate. The hair-drier should be on the lowest heat setting.

6. Using a timer, keep track of how long it takes for each sponge to completely dry. Which sponge dries the quickest? Which dries the slowest?

Helpful Hint: The heat from the hair-drier mimics the Sun's heat.

Hardworking plants

Evaporation isn't the only process that changes liquid water into gaseous water. Transpiration is a cycle too. Plant roots pull water from the ground. Tiny pores on the leaves called stomata release gaseous water vapour into the air. Try this simple experiment to see how transpiration works.

FACT

Transpiration is often an invisible process. Roughly half a hectare (1 acre) of corn contributes between 11,400 and 15,100 litres of water into the atmosphere every day. A large tree can transpire 151,400 litres of water per year!

What you need

small pot plant

cling film

twist tie

petroleum jelly

glass jar

timer or clock

What you do

1. Cover the pot, the soil and the base of the plant with cling film. Make sure it is as airtight as possible. Do not wrap the plant itself.

2. Use the twist tie to hold the cling film tightly to the plant's stem.

3. Smear petroleum jelly around the rim of the jar's mouth. Carefully place the jar upside down over the plant. Push against the cling film to form a tight seal.

4. Put the plant in the sunshine. Observe the plant for 30 to 60 minutes. What do you notice happening inside the jar? Are there water droplets on the inside of the jar?

Clouds and condensation

Water vapour in the atmosphere is the key ingredient of rain-making clouds. Vapour high in the atmosphere cools and forms water droplets. But what holds the droplets in the sky long enough to form a cloud?

The "glue" that helps the droplets form comes from tiny dust particles floating in the atmosphere. Droplets cling to the dust, which forms a cloud. When enough droplets gather together, they become heavy enough to drop to Earth as rain or snow. See how this process of condensation works with your own cloud-making experiment.

Types of cloud

There are many types of cloud. **Stratus clouds** are low horizontal clouds that blanket the sky. Stratus clouds usually mean rain or snow is on the way. Puffy vertical clouds are called **cumulus clouds**. When they turn from white and puffy to dark gray, rain is likely to fall. On a nice day you may see wispy **cirrus clouds**. They are formed from ice crystals high in the sky. **Nimbus clouds** have snow or rain falling from them. Clouds can also be combinations of various types. A cumulonimbus cloud, for example, is a puffy cloud with rain falling from it.

stratus cloud   low cloud that forms over a large area; stratus clouds often bring light rain

cumulus cloud   white, puffy cloud with a flat, rounded base

cirrus cloud   high, thin cloud made of ice crystals that looks like strands of white silk

nimbus cloud   cloud that produces precipitation

What you do

1. Pour hot water into a jar until the water is about 2.5 centimetres (1 in) high. Swish it around to warm the inside of the jar.

2. Place two ice cubes in the jar's upside-down lid. Place the upside-down lid with the ice cubes in it on top of the jar.

3. Hold a piece of dark paper behind the jar. This will help you see condensation beginning to form on the jar.

Safety First!

Ask an adult to help when using hot water and matches.

4. Ask an adult to light the matches while you lift the lid off the jar. Ask an adult to put the matches into the jar. Quickly put the lid back on the jar.

5. With the dark paper in place, watch a swirling cloud begin to form! How do you think the cloud formed? Where can you see condensation?

Shimmering rainbow

The water that collects in clouds eventually becomes raindrops or snowflakes. Sometimes when conditions are right, this precipitation in the air produces a rainbow. As sunlight passes through raindrops, the light slows down and bends. The **wavelengths** of light separate into rainbow colours. But you don't have to wait for a rain shower to see a rainbow. Follow these steps to create your own!

wavelength distance between two peaks of a wave of light or sound

What you do

What you need

small mirror

glass large enough to fit the mirror inside

water

torch

1. Place a small mirror inside a glass. Lean the mirror against one side of the glass so it is slightly angled.

2. Fill the glass with water until the mirror is completely under water.

Rainbow colours

When you see a rainbow, it looks like a giant arch. But a rainbow is actually a complete circle. If conditions are right, you can see a complete rainbow from an aeroplane. You'll always see the colour red on the outer edge of a rainbow. Red is the colour with the longest wavelength. Red is followed by orange, yellow, green, blue, indigo and then violet. The phrase "Richard Of York Gave Battle in Vain" can be used to help remember the first letter of each of the colours in order.

3. Put the glass on the floor in a very dark room. Make sure all outside light is blocked.

4. Shine a torch through the glass at a slight angle from the mirror. Where can you see a rainbow?

21

Incredible edible aquifer

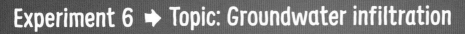

Some rain finds its way to streams and rivers and is eventually carried out to sea. But some rain seeps into the ground where it fills underground **aquifers**. The water is cleaned by the soil and stored underground. Some of the water is pumped to the surface and is used as drinking water. With this project you can build your own aquifer – and eat it too!

aquifer   underground layer of rock or soil which is able to hold and transmit water

Aquifer

Aquifers are a great source of fresh drinking water and are very useful for crop irrigation. In the form of precipitation, water can re-enter an aquifer to refill its empty spaces.

What you do

What you need

large, clear glass

small gummy bears

chocolate chips

crushed ice cubes

clear lemonade

ice cream

sprinkles

drinking straw

1. Fill a clear glass one-third full with a combination of gummy bears, chocolate chips and crushed ice. These small items represent soil and dirt that make up an aquifer.

2. Add the lemonade until the gummy bears, chocolate chips and crushed ice are covered. The lemonade is groundwater and fills the spaces between the soil and rocks.

3. Add a scoop of ice cream to the cup. The ice cream is a **confining layer** above the aquifer and protects the water from being contaminated.

4. Pour sprinkles on top of the ice cream. The sprinkles represent soil, which is **porous** and allows water to seep through.

5. "Drill" a **well** into your aquifer with a straw. Begin to pump the well by slowly sucking on the straw. What happens to the lemonade groundwater?

6. Recharge the aquifer by adding a bit more lemonade, also known as precipitation. Where does the lemonade go?

confining layer layer of rock or clay between Earth's surface and an underground aquifer; water does not easily seep through a confining layer

porous having tiny holes through which gas or liquid may pass through

well deep hole dug into the ground to obtain water

Make your own drinking water

Is it possible for Earth to run out of drinking water? Safe drinking water is in short supply in many places on Earth. One reason is that most of the water on the planet is salty sea water. Humans cannot drink salt water. But a simple tool based on a natural process can make salt water drinkable. Try this **desalination** project for yourself.

Very little water on Earth is fresh enough to drink. Of the 2 per cent of freshwater on Earth, most is frozen in glaciers.

desalinate process of removing salt from water

What you do

What you need

- measuring jug
- drinking water
- large metal or glass mixing bowl
- table salt
- spoon
- heavy drinking glass that is shorter than the mixing bowl
- cling film
- small rock
- clock or timer

Safety First!

Never taste ingredients used in experiments unless instructed.

1. Pour 1 litre of water into a mixing bowl.

2. Add 30 grams (2 tablespoons) salt, and stir with the spoon until the salt is dissolved in the water. Dip a clean finger in the salty water and taste it.

   Helpful Hint: Make sure all supplies used in this project are clean and sanitary.

3. Place a drinking glass inside the bowl, and centre the glass in the bowl.

4. Stretch cling film over the bowl. Make sure the top of the bowl is completely covered and the film is tightly sealed to the bowl.

5. Put a rock on the cling film directly above the glass. Make sure the cling film doesn't touch the top of the glass.

6. Place the bowl in the sunshine or under an incandescent lamp for two hours.

7. Carefully remove the rock and the cling film. Remove the drinking glass and taste the water inside it. Does the water taste salty?

The most important liquid on the planet

Water is the most precious and life-sustaining resource on Earth. Without it life could not exist. Next time you drink a glass of water, think about all the places it has been. Think of all the ways it plays a role in your life. And think of the fun you've had experimenting with Earth's natural processes relating to water!

Glossary

aquifer underground layer of rock or soil which is able to hold and transmit water

atmosphere mixture of gases that surrounds Earth

cirrus cloud high, thin cloud made of ice crystals that looks like strands of white silk

condense change from a gas to a liquid

confining layer layer of rock or clay between Earth's surface and an underground aquifer; water does not easily seep through a confining layer

cumulus cloud white, puffy cloud with a flat, rounded base

desalinate process of removing salt from water

evaporate change from a liquid to a vapour or a gas

nimbus cloud cloud that produces precipitation

porous having tiny holes through which gas or liquid may pass through

precipitation water that falls from clouds to Earth's surface

stratus cloud low cloud that forms over a large area; stratus clouds often bring light rain

transpiration process in which plants give off moisture into the atmosphere

vapour gas made from something that is usually a liquid or solid at normal temperatures

water cycle how water changes as it travels around the world and moves between the ground and the air

wavelength distance between two peaks of a wave of light or sound

well deep hole dug into the ground to obtain water

Read more

Living Beside a River (Places We Live), Ellen Labrecque (Raintree, 2015)

Seas (Explorer Travel Guides), Nick Hunter (Raintree, 2014)

Weather (The Science Behind), Darlene R. Stille (Raintree, 2013)

Websites

www.bbc.co.uk/bitesize/ks2/science/materials/
Explore the changing states of materials on Earth through games, quizzes, diagrams and film.

http://ngkids.co.uk/science-and-nature/water-cycle
Did you know that Earth has been recycling water for over 4 billion years? For more information about the water cycle and some amazing water facts and figures, visit the National Geographic children's website.

Index